Christians in a Hostile World

Christians in a Hostile World

by
John MacArthur, Jr.

"GRACE TO YOU"
P.O. Box 4000
Panorama City, CA   91412

All Scripture quotations, unless noted otherwise, are from the *New
American Standard Bible*, © 1960, 1962, 1963, 1968, 1971, 1972, 1973, 1975,
and 1977 by The Lockman Foundation, and are used by permission.

ISBN: 0-8024-5328-7

1 2 3 4 5 Printing/LC/Year 95 94 93 92 91

Printed in the United States of America

Contents

These Bible studies are taken from messages delivered by Pastor-Teacher John MacArthur, Jr., at Grace Community Church in Sun Valley, California. These messages have been combined into a 6-tape album titled *Christians in a Hostile World*. You may purchase this series either in an attractive vinyl cassette album or as individual cassettes. To purchase these tapes, request the album *Christians in a Hostile World*, or ask for the tapes by their individual GC numbers. Please consult the current price list; then send your order, making your check payable to:

Word of Grace
24900 Anza Drive
Santa Clarita, CA 91355

Or call the following toll-free number:
1-800-55-GRACE

1

Securities Against a Hostile World

Outline

Introduction
A. A Believer's Identity in a Hostile World
B. A Believer's Relationship to a Hostile World
C. A Believer's Perspective in a Hostile World

Lesson
I.   A Passion for Goodness (v. 13)
     A. A Rhetorical Question
     B. A Pure Life
II. A Willingness to Suffer (v. 14)
     A. The Possibility of Suffering
         1. Peter spoke about it
         2. Christ experienced it
     B. The Privilege of Suffering
         1. It brings blessing from God
         2. It illustrates the importance of fearing God
III. A Devotion to Christ (v. 15a)
IV. A Readiness to Defend the Faith (v. 15b)
     A. What a Believer Should Answer
     B. How a Believer Should Answer
V.   A Pure Conscience (v. 16)

Conclusion

Introduction

The apostle Peter gave essential instructions to believers about living in a hostile world. Because believers in those days were undergoing severe persecution, Peter wanted them to live securely in the midst of hostility. He begins directly addressing the issue of persecution in 1 Peter 3:13. But before that, he gave some important spiritual advice.

A. A Believer's Identity in a Hostile World

First, Peter wanted the persecuted believers to know their identity as Christians (1 Pet. 1:1–2:12). At the beginning of this section he identified them as "chosen" (1:1), and toward the end he identified them as "a chosen race, a royal priesthood, a holy nation, a people for God's own possession" (2:9). Knowing their identity encouraged the believers to "proclaim the excellencies" of God, who called them out of sin to live righteously.

Peter also pointed out that believers are "aliens and strangers" (v. 11). A believer is a foreigner and pilgrim living without a permanent home or citizenship. He only lives in this world temporarily and does not participate in its ungodliness. Peter said, "Keep your behavior excellent among the [unsaved], so that . . . they may on account of your good deeds, as they observe them, glorify God in the day of visitation" (v. 12). The Lord uses holy lives to draw the lost to Christ. When unbelievers become Christians, they glorify God.

B. A Believer's Relationship to a Hostile World

Believers are to have proper relationships with others, in part to evangelize the lost (1 Pet. 2:13–3:12). That involves how we relate to those in positions of authority (2:13-20), our spouses (3:1-7), other believers (3:8-13), and so on.

C. A Believer's Perspective in a Hostile World

After speaking about our identity in Christ and our relationship to society, Peter explains how to live securely in an unfriendly society. A believer needs to arm himself with a trust in the power of righteousness to triumph over persecution and suffering. During times of hostility, we're to have confidence, not get caught up in turmoil.

The early church experienced great persecution, but that's not the case for the contemporary church in most of the world. Physical persecution exists in some places, but in our nation it's not usually overt or aggressive. However, there seems to be a mounting hostility toward Christianity in our society. Many non-Christians treat immorality as an alternate lifestyle and believe man can solve his problems in whatever way he chooses. Christians in our nation can expect to face increasing hostility on personal and governmental fronts.

First Peter 3:13-17 is for every godly believer who lives in an ungodly culture. It tells us how to defend ourselves against hostile threats and silence false accusations. So let's look at what keeps the believer secure against a hostile world.

Lesson

I. A PASSION FOR GOODNESS (v. 13)

"Who is there to harm you if you prove zealous for what is good?"

A. A Rhetorical Question

Most people find it difficult to mistreat those who are fervent in doing good. Those who love to do good are often gracious, unselfish, kind, loving, and caring. But frauds who steal from widows and orphans aren't usually well-liked. Even the ungodly condemn those who make themselves rich at the expense of others. So

Peter lays down a general principle: A person who is generous and thoughtful to others isn't often the object of hostility. The implied answer to his rhetorical question is that few would harm a believer who does good.

B. A Pure Life

"Prove" means "to become," a reference to a person's character. "Zealous" refers to intensity and enthusiasm. During New Testament times a fanatical group of patriots called the Zealots pledged to free Israel from foreign rule. Simon the Zealot, one of the apostles, probably belonged to that group. Peter wanted all his readers to be zealots in the sense of doing good. A passion for doing good produces a pure life, which should be the goal and delight of every believer. When a believer is consumed with godly living, he will lose his appetite for the world's ungodly attractions.

The words "If you should suffer for the sake of righteousness" (1 Pet. 3:14) imply that a passion for goodness isn't a guarantee against persecution. Doing good simply reduces the likelihood of persecution. No one did more good than Jesus, yet a hostile world eventually killed Him. Nevertheless, a believer's life should be above reproach so critics will have no just reason for their accusations.

II. A WILLINGNESS TO SUFFER (v. 14)

"But even if you should suffer for the sake of righteousness, you are blessed. And do not fear their intimidation, and do not be troubled."

A. The Possibility of Suffering

"But even if" conveys the idea of "perchance" or "contrary to what is expected." The verb "should suffer" indicates the remote possibility that one will suffer for doing good. Peter said that whereas suffering for doing good isn't likely to happen, it can happen. Indeed, many Christians suffered for their obedience to Christ in the early church, but others undoubtedly suffered for their disobedience. When a Christian disobeys God's

10

Word, the world senses a greater justification and freedom for its hostility. But even godly Christians should not be surprised or afraid when suffering happens.

1. Peter spoke about it

Later in the text Peter says, "Beloved, do not be surprised at the fiery ordeal among you, which comes upon you for your testing, as though some strange thing were happening to you; but to the degree that you share the sufferings of Christ, keep on rejoicing; so that also at the revelation of His glory, you may rejoice with exultation. If you are reviled for the name of Christ, you are blessed, because the Spirit of glory and of God rests upon you. By no means let any of you suffer as a murderer, or thief, or evildoer, or a troublesome meddler; but if anyone suffers as a Christian, let him not feel ashamed, but in that name let him glorify God" (4:12-16). A believer is to accept suffering in his life because God has a spiritual purpose for it.

2. Christ experienced it

As mentioned before, even the sinless Christ suffered persecution: "Christ . . . suffered for you, leaving you an example for you to follow in His steps, who committed no sin, nor was any deceit found in His mouth; and while being reviled, He did not revile in return; while suffering, He uttered no threats, but kept entrusting Himself to Him who judges righteously" (2:21-23). Believers can identify with and intimately know "the fellowship of [Christ's] sufferings" (Phil. 3:10).

B. The Privilege of Suffering

1. It brings blessing from God

Sometimes unbelievers can't tolerate a righteous man or woman. A holy life irritates them to the point of aggression. A believer who suffers under such circumstances is "blessed" (1 Pet. 3:14). "Blessed"

11

doesn't emphasize happiness or joy as much as it does the meaning of "privilege" or "honor." Elizabeth said Mary the mother of Jesus was "blessed among women" (Luke 1:42). Mary's heart was pierced with many sorrows (Luke 2:35), so that isn't a reference to general happiness. Instead, it speaks of divine favor —the privilege of giving birth to the Messiah in Mary's case. A believer has the same sense of privilege when he shares in Christ's sufferings.

Perhaps Peter learned the meaning of "blessed" from our Lord's words in Matthew 5:10-12: "Blessed are those who have been persecuted for the sake of righteousness, for theirs is the kingdom of heaven. Blessed are you when men cast insults at you, and persecute you, and say all kinds of evil against you falsely, on account of Me. Rejoice, and be glad, for your reward in heaven is great." A believer has the honor of receiving a divine, eternal reward for suffering on Christ's behalf.

2. It illustrates the importance of fearing God

The last part of 1 Peter 3:14 alludes to Isaiah 8:12-13: "You are not to fear what they fear or be in dread of it. It is the Lord of hosts whom you should regard as holy. And He shall be your fear, and He shall be your dread."

In the days of the prophet Isaiah, Ahaz king of Judah faced a crisis in the face of the Assyrian army's impending invasion. The kings of Israel and Syria wanted Ahaz to join them in an alliance against the Assyrian forces, but Ahaz refused. Because he refused, Israel and Syria threatened to invade Judah. Behind the scenes Ahaz had made an alliance with Assyria, but Isaiah warned Ahaz against that ungodly alliance and told him not to fear. Isaiah meant either that Ahaz was not to fear as Syria and Israel did, or that he was not to fear the enemy's intimidation. Instead, the king was to fear the Lord and thereby not be troubled or shaken.

12

In the same sense, a Christian isn't to be shaken by whatever hostilities threaten him. Fearing the Lord will help him face opposition with courage and see suffering as an opportunity for spiritual blessings, not as an opportunity to compromise his faith before the unbelieving world. As Martin Luther stood before his accusers and refused to recant his beliefs, so Christians today must stand firm in the faith. Church history reveals that many Christians lost their lives because they refused to compromise their stand for the Lord.

To be dedicated to the Lord in the face of persecution demands that our minds and affections be set on heavenly values, not earthly ones. A believer preoccupied with possessions, pleasures, and popularity will fear the enemy's assault. But the heavenly-minded believer can "count it all joy" when he encounters various trials (James 1:2, KJV*).

III. A DEVOTION TO CHRIST (v. 15a)

"Sanctify Christ as Lord in your hearts."

Peter again alludes to Isaiah 8:13, which says, "Sanctify the Lord" (KJV). Whereas Isaiah used the word *Lord,* Peter used the words *Christ as Lord*. Peter meant that regardless of the opposition a believer may face, he always is to affirm in his heart that Christ is Lord. He is to accept and acknowledge the Lord's sovereignty and majesty, fearing only Him.

"To sanctify" indicates adoring, exalting, magnifying, and giving primary place to something. The believer who sanctifies Christ exalts Him as the object of his love and loyalty. The believer recognizes His perfection, magnifies His glory, and extols His greatness. He submits himself to God's will, realizing that His will sometimes includes suffering. To live that way is to "adorn the doctrine of God

---

*King James Version.

13

our Savior in every respect" (Titus 2:10). The Christian, in the deepest part of his or her being, is committed to honoring Christ as Lord—even in the midst of suffering. Submission to Christ as Lord yields courage, boldness, and fortitude in the midst of hostility.

IV. A READINESS TO DEFEND THE FAITH (v. 15b)

"Always being ready to make a defense to everyone who asks you to give an account for the hope that is in you, yet with gentleness and reverence."

A. What a Believer Should Answer

When society attacks, the believer is to be prepared to make a "defense" (Gk., *apologia*, from which the English words *apology* and *apologetic* are derived). The Greek term often means a formal defense in a court of law. Paul used it to describe his defense in a courtroom (2 Tim. 4:16). And Festus, the governor of Judea, used it the same way to explain Paul's case to King Agrippa (Acts 25:16).

But Paul also used *apologia* informally to describe being able to answer anyone who questioned him (Phil. 1:16-17)—not just a judge, magistrate, or governor. Furthermore, "always" in 1 Peter 3:15 indicates that a believer should be prepared to answer in all situations, not just in the legal sphere. So the use of "defense" in 1 Peter 3:15 is general: Whether formally in an official setting or informally to anyone who might inquire, a believer is to be ready to provide an answer. That answer is about "the hope that is in you," which refers to the Christian faith. Believers should be able to give a rational explanation of their salvation and Christian faith.

B. How a Believer Should Answer

A Christian is to explain his faith "with gentleness and reverence." That indicates a tender and a gracious spirit in speaking. "Gentleness" speaks of meekness or humility, both references to power under control. "Reverence" (Gk., *phobeō*) means "fear." *Phobia* is a derivative of that

14

Greek word. But this kind of fear refers to a healthy devotion to God, a healthy regard for truth, and a healthy respect for the person being spoken to. Therefore, a believer isn't to be quarrelsome when sharing his faith (2 Tim. 2:24-26).

A Christian who can't carefully, thoughtfully, reasonably, and biblically give a clear explanation for his faith will be insecure when faced with hostility and might be inclined to doubt his salvation. The enemy's blows will devastate those who haven't "put on the breastplate of faith and love, and as a helmet, the hope of salvation" (1 Thess. 5:8).

V.   A PURE CONSCIENCE (v. 16)

"Keep a good conscience so that in the thing in which you are slandered, those who revile your good behavior in Christ may be put to shame."

"Keep" means "to maintain" or "possess." The conscience either accuses or excuses a person, acting as a source of conviction or affirmation. "A good conscience" is one that doesn't accuse a believer of sin because he or she is living a godly life. A good conscience says everything is well, but an evil conscience points out sin in a person's life.

A believer is to live with a clear conscience so the weight of guilt won't burden him when he faces hostile criticism. However, if he doesn't have a passion for doing good or serving Christ as Lord, he will know the heavy weight of deserved guilt. A defiled conscience can't be at ease or withstand the onslaught of trials. But a clear conscience will help a believer not to be anxious or troubled in his trials. That's one of the reasons Paul said, "I . . . do my best to maintain always a blameless conscience both before God and before men" (Acts 24:16).

A pure conscience provides tranquillity and vindicates the slandered believer. His conscience won't point out any sin, and his godly life will prove any criticisms to be false. Accusations against a believer should be for his doing good, not evil (1 Pet. 2:12; 4:14-16). "Slandered" refers to verbal abuse, and "revile" means "to threaten, insult, or mistreat." When a believer has a pure conscience, the verbal abuse and insults against him bring shame to the accuser, not the believer.

The world self-righteously condemns Christianity when it can point to a Christian who has scandalized the faith. Unbelievers enjoy drawing attention to a sinning Christian because they want to justify their sinful behavior. Therefore all Christians are to live above reproach so that no accusations have a valid basis.

Conclusion

First Peter 3:17 says, "It is better, if God should will it so, that you suffer for doing what is right rather than for doing what is wrong." A believer has two options. The first is to do right, even if it results in suffering. A believer is to accept suffering as part of God's wise and sovereign plan for his or her life. The second option is to choose to do wrong, which will result in suffering. Both options are according to God's will. God wills a believer to suffer for doing right so that he receives spiritual strength and glorifies God, and God wills that a believer suffer divine chastisement for doing wrong. So do good, and avoid bringing suffering upon yourself from doing wrong.

Focusing on the Facts

1. How does Peter identify believers (1 Pet. 1:1; 2:9, 11; see p. 8)?
2. What relationships does 1 Peter 2:13–3:13 talk about (see p. 8)?
3. Explain the implied answer to the question in 1 Peter 3:13 (see p. 9).
4. What is the spiritual result of being zealous in godly living (see p. 10)?
5. What are two indications that suffering is possible for the believer? Explain (see p. 11).
6. What does "blessed" mean in 1 Peter 3:14 (see pp. 11-12)?

7. What lesson did Peter teach from the life of Ahaz (Isa. 8:12-13; 1 Pet. 3:14; see pp. 12-13)?
8. What does being dedicated to the Lord demand (see p. 13)?
9. What does "sanctify Christ as Lord" mean (1 Pet. 3:15; see pp. 13-14)?
10. What does "defense" mean in 1 Peter 3:15 (see p. 14)?
11. Explain what defense the believer should be always ready to give (1 Pet. 3:15; see p. 14).
12. What danger exists for a believer who isn't ready to give a defense (see pp. 14-15)?
13. What is a "good conscience" (1 Pet. 3:16)? How does it help a believer who faces criticism (see p. 15)?
14. What are two options in a believer's life (1 Peter 3:17)? How are both within God's will (see p. 16)?

Pondering the Principles

1. First Peter 3:14 indicates that suffering is a spiritual privilege for a believer. If a Christian knows "that God causes all things to work together for good" (Rom. 8:28), he will be able to accept suffering as part of God's plan for his life. Puritan Thomas Watson said, "Afflictions work for good, as they make way for glory. . . . Not that they merit glory, but they prepare for it. As ploughing prepares the earth for a crop, so afflictions prepare and make us [ready] for glory. The painter lays his gold upon dark colours, so God first lays the dark colours of affliction, and then He lays the golden colour of glory. The vessel is first seasoned before wine is poured into it: the vessels of mercy are first seasoned with affliction, and then the wine of glory is poured in. Thus we see afflictions are not prejudicial, but beneficial, to the saints" (*All Things for Good* [Edinburgh: The Banner of Truth Trust, 1986], p. 32). When you face suffering, be encouraged knowing it's working for your spiritual benefit. If you know someone who is going through difficult times, take time to encourage him or her through God's Word.

2. Scripture charges the believer to explain his faith "with gentleness and reverence" (1 Pet. 3:15). Read the following verses, and write down what they teach about godly speaking habits:

   - Proverbs 15:1; 17:27
   - Proverbs 12:18; 15:4; Ephesians 4:31
   - Proverbs 10:18; 16:28; Colossians 3:8-9
   - Proverbs 13:3; 17:28
   - Proverbs 15:7; 16:23; Ephesians 4:29
   - Proverbs 16:24; 25:11; Colossians 4:6
   - Proverbs 19:22; Ephesians 4:25

2

The Christian's Duty in a Hostile World—Part 1

Outline

Introduction
A. The Church's Spiritual Condition
   1. In the past
   2. At the present
      a) A new basis of faith
      b) A new object of affection
      c) A new goal in life
B. A Christian's Spiritual Motivation

Lesson
I.   The Incentive (v. 7*a*)
   A. The Imminence of Christ's Return
   B. The Presence of the Last Days
      1. The early church was already in the last days
      2. The last days began with Christ's first coming
   C. The Godly Effect of Expecting Christ's Return

Conclusion

Introduction

The church today urgently needs spiritual revival. That will occur only when Christians fulfill their spiritual duty. When we do, the church will have a greater spiritual impact on the lost world.

A. The Church's Spiritual Condition

1. In the past

Not long ago the church experienced a revival. The Jesus movement of the 1970s yielded an unprecedented rise in conservative biblical evangelicalism. During that time there was a great interest in evangelism, Bible study, and discipleship. New Bible translations appeared, and Christian broadcasting, publishing, and music ministries expanded rapidly. Churches experienced rapid numerical growth, and some built auditoriums that could seat several thousand people.

2. At the present

However, the prevailing trend now in the church is a departure from that Spirit-moved revival. The church has become a popularized institution. As it continues to eliminate every offense from its message, the church has increased its social acceptance. Now it is characterized by self-centeredness, secular psychology, and pragmatism. Today's church asks, Does it work? What will it do for me? How much success will it bring? How much money will it make? But instead it should be asking, What honors the heart of God?

This "pop church" is found on "Christian" television, radio, and celebrity variety shows. Entertainment has replaced worship, pride has replaced humility, success has replaced excellence, and cleverness has replaced character. Sometimes Christian radio shows feature guests who make unbiblical claims about God, yet the host makes no attempt to correct them. Psychology and psychiatry have replaced Bible teaching as the staple of Christian radio. And local churches are becoming comfort zones, Christian country clubs, and community centers, with little redemptive impact or threat against sin. Several main features categorize this popular Christianity.

a) A new basis of faith

Its trend is more subtle than theological liberal-
ism, which directly attacks the church and therefore is easy to see and deal with. The popular
church pretends to adhere to the truth, yet quiet-
ly undermines it. It substitutes experience, emotion, and problem-solving for the Word of God
as its basis of faith. Its theology is focused on
meeting people's needs. The charismatic movement is at the forefront of this new basis of faith,
with its emphasis on private revelations, prophe-
cies, and visions. Many Christian ministries are
now characterized by pragmatism, manipulation,
and consumerism.

b) A new object of affection

Instead of Christ as the object of affection, the
popular church is attracted to a celebrity, an
evangelist, a project, a fund-raising campaign, a
new building, or supposed miracles and healings.
Faith has turned to fantasy with a message of
health, wealth, and comfort. In that kind of environment "easy believism" flourishes, so many
people who associate themselves with the church
aren't even Christians.

In the contemporary church much of the emphasis is on solving one's own problems so one
can live more comfortably, and there is little
focus on Christ's second coming because that
would end the pursuit of pleasure and prosperi-
ty. So we have to ask, Where is Christ-centered
faith that helps a believer stand in the midst of
his trials? Emotionalism is selfish escapism, not
biblical faith.

c) A new goal in life

The new goal is happiness and satisfaction, not
holiness. Whatever makes a person happy is
what he or she is encouraged to pursue.

21

Each one of those features negatively affects the church's spiritual vitality, and they are Satan's attempts to destroy the church.

How can the church have revival? What should its focus be? How can it be useful to God and not lose its power? First Peter 4:7-11 answers those questions.

B. A Christian's Spiritual Motivation

Several motivating factors help a Christian to be faithful during times of suffering. First, every believer has a precious salvation that demands his or her best effort (1 Pet. 1:1–2:10). Second, he should live a holy life because God has called him to be a witness for Christ, no matter how difficult it is (1 Pet. 2:11–4:6). Third, he is to live with Christ's second coming in view, not his difficult circumstances (1 Pet. 4:7–5:11). Those are the basic motives for living the Christian life.

In his present situation the believer has certain securities against a hostile world (1 Pet. 3:13-17; see pp. 9-16). But in the midst of suffering, what is his duty and what is his incentive for doing it?

Lesson

I. THE INCENTIVE (v. 7a)

"The end of all things is at hand."

The Greek term translated "end" (*telos*) doesn't necessarily refer to cessation, termination, or some kind of chronological end. The term speaks of consummation, a goal achieved, a purpose attained, or fulfillment. The consummation in view here is Christ's second coming. If it were the consummation of persecution, we might assume an imminent change in government rule whereby its citizens receive benevolent treatment. But this is the consummation of "all things." The second coming is the only time when all things will be consummated. Peter referred to that event

22

when he said believers are protected by God's power "for a salvation ready to be revealed in the last time" (1 Pet. 1:5)—"at the revelation of Jesus Christ" (v. 7).

A. The Imminence of Christ's Return

The verb translated "is at hand" means coming near. Its perfect tense indicates a process consummated with a resulting nearness. That means the event is imminent—it could happen at any moment. A believer is to live with an attitude of anticipation or expectancy because Christ's return is imminent. Anticipating His return is a mark of faithfulness. Many New Testament passages reflect that truth.

1. 1 Thessalonians 1:10—We're "to wait for [God's] Son from heaven, whom He raised from the dead, that is Jesus, who delivers us from the wrath to come." Paul commended the Thessalonian believers because they were waiting for Jesus Christ to return from heaven. Waiting creates a pilgrim, or sojourner, mentality, reminding us that we are foreigners in this world, with a heavenly citizenship.

2. Acts 1:7—Jesus said, "It is not for you to know times or epochs which the Father has fixed by His own authority." God hasn't chosen to tell us when Jesus will come. If we knew the time of Christ's return, it would affect our motivation. If we knew He wasn't coming soon, we would become lazy. On the other hand, if we knew He was coming soon, we'd probably panic. But imminence eliminates both reactions, so we can live in expectancy.

3. Matthew 24:36—Jesus said, "Of that day and hour no one knows, not even the angels of heaven, nor the Son, but the Father alone." Even in His incarnation, Christ didn't know the time of His return. Only the Father knows that time.

   Christ's imminent return is an unpopular doctrine, which most people today aren't interested in. In fact, one of the compelling reasons people today teach a post-Tribulation rapture is that the time scheme allows for plenty of warning prior to His return. They assert that Christ won't return until the end of the seven-year Tribulation. Consequently, they say believers will live through the Tribulation period.

If a believer were to know he would live through the Tribulation period, that would remove the pressure of expectancy that holds him to a high level of accountability now. He would be tempted to think he could live any way he wanted. During the Tribulation he'd recognize the abomination of desolation in Jerusalem when a sacrifice on the Temple altar is made; he'd know when the seals are broken and the terrible plagues begin; he'd see when the waters turn to blood. If a believer charted his way through that period, he'd have a good idea of when Christ would return and perhaps delay being obedient.

But Christ could return at any moment (1 Pet. 4:7), and when He does He will be "ready to judge the living and the dead" (v. 5). So a believer is accountable for holy living because he expects Christ to come at any moment as Judge. Although the wait for His return might appear to be long, we know "that with the Lord one day is as a thousand years, and a thousand years as one day" (2 Pet. 3:8).

4. 1 Corinthians 15:51-53—Paul said, "I tell you a mystery; we shall not all sleep, but we shall all be changed, in a moment, in the twinkling of an eye, at the last trumpet; for the trumpet will sound, and the dead will be raised imperishable, and we shall be changed. For this perishable must put on the imperishable, and this mortal must put on immortality."

The Lord will clothe a believer in immortality within the time it takes to refract light off the pupil. The happening is not only sudden but also a mystery, which indicates it hasn't already been revealed. The sounding trumpet signifies Christ's imminent return, which is when the change occurs.

5. 1 Thessalonians 4:15-17—Paul said, "This we say to you by the word of the Lord, that we who are alive, and remain until the coming of the Lord, shall not precede those who have fallen asleep. For the Lord Himself will descend from heaven with a shout, with the voice of the archangel, and with the trumpet of God; and the dead in Christ shall rise first. Then we who are alive and remain shall be caught up together with them in the clouds to meet the Lord in the air, and thus we shall always be with the Lord."

"By the word of the Lord" means a revelation from the Lord Himself about the rapture. And "we" indicates that Paul expected the Lord's return in his lifetime. The church is responsible to live in the light His return.

6. James 5:7-8—"Be patient, therefore, brethren, until the coming of the Lord. Behold, the farmer waits for the precious produce of the soil, being patient about it, until it gets the early and late rains. You too be patient; strengthen your hearts, for the coming of the Lord is at hand."

Since the believers were undergoing persecution, James encouraged them to patiently wait for the Lord's return. Obviously Christ didn't return then, but nevertheless the persecuted believers were to live in that expectancy. "Is at hand" speaks of imminence. The reality that Jesus could come at any moment should always be on the heart of every believer.

7. Hebrews 10:25—We should not be "forsaking our own assembling together, as is the habit of some, but encouraging one another; and all the more, as you see the day drawing near." Believers are to gather together faithfully to comfort each other. The Hebrews were motivated to do so because the time of Lord's return was approaching. Since we are living about two thousand years after the letter's writing, there is even more urgency now to gather with God's people.

8. Hebrews 12:26-27—In Haggai 2:6 God tells the prophet Haggai that He will remove this material world and establish His eternal kingdom and glory: "'Yet once more I will shake not only the earth, but also the heaven.' And this expression, 'Yet once more,' denotes the removing of those things which can be shaken, as of created things, in order that those things which cannot be shaken may remain." We are to live in light of our glorious future as those in New Testament times did.

9. Revelation 1:3—"Blessed is he who reads and those who hear the words of the prophecy, and heed the things which are written in it; for the time is near." A believer receives divine approval for reading the book of Revelation and observing its content because the Lord could return at any moment.

10. Revelation 22:20—The apostle John said, "He who testifies to these things says, 'Yes, I am coming quickly.' Amen. Come, Lord Jesus." God's Word says that Christ's coming will be speedy, to which John added his agreement because he too lived in the anticipation of Christ's imminent return.

B. The Presence of the Last Days

1. The early church was already in the last days

First John 2:18 says, "It is the last hour." The apostle John was already living in the last days when he wrote his letter. Second Timothy 3:1 says, "In the last days difficult times will come." The apostle Paul gave a detailed description of people who characterize the last days since the church was already in that time frame. First Timothy 4:1 says, "The Spirit explicitly says that in later times some will fall away from the faith." Departure from the faith was already happening in the early church, so the Spirit was specific in describing it.

2. The last days began with Christ's first coming

   a) John 19:30—Jesus said, "It is finished!" The Jewish people who lived during the days of Christ saw the Old Covenant end and the inauguration of the New Covenant. The whole system of ceremonies, rituals, sacrifices, priests, and offerings collapsed with the tearing of the Temple veil and the opening of the Holy of Holies to everyone (Matt. 27:51; Heb. 10:14-22). Later, God sent judgment via the Romans to destroy Jerusalem and the Temple. That ended the sacrificial system even to this day. When Jesus was on the cross, He completed the inauguration of the New Covenant. Beforehand He declared, "Not one [Temple] stone here shall be left upon another, which will not be torn down" (Matt. 24:2). The Temple's destruction symbolized the devastation of the entire Old Testament economy. The old order ended, and the new order of the Messiah began.

   b) Hebrews 9:26-28—"At the consummation of the ages [Christ] has been manifested to put away sin by the sacrifice of Himself. And inasmuch as it is appointed for men to die once and after this comes judgment, so Christ also, having been offered once to bear the sins of many, shall appear a second time for salvation without reference to sin, to those who eagerly await Him."

   Christ's first coming "at the consummation of the ages" provided salvation through His death on the cross. Taking us out of the kingdom of darkness and placing us into the kingdom of His Son, God provided redemption and forgiveness for our sins (Col. 1:13-14). Christ established His authority and began to build His kingdom, having defeated sin and death. We are living in the last days of that spiritual and inward kingdom. On the other hand, Christ's second coming will be to establish His earthly kingdom. With His incarnation the kingdom came in a state of grace, but when He returns, it will come in a state of glory.

27

Christ's death, resurrection, and exaltation to the Father's right hand brought in the dawn of a new era. The Messiah's kingdom exists now as a spiritual reality and will soon appear in its visible form.

C. The Godly Effect of Expecting Christ's Return

Christ's imminent coming should lead us to a godly attitude and holy living, not turn us into zealous fanatics or lazy dreamers who do nothing but lie around. Scripture indicates that His coming should make us watchful pursuers of righteousness.

1. 2 Corinthians 5:9-10—"We have as our ambition, whether at home or absent, to be pleasing to Him. For we must all appear before the judgment seat of Christ, that each one may be recompensed for his deeds in the body, according to what he has done, whether good or bad."

   The mark of every true Christian is a desire to please Christ. Not wanting to please Him indicates an absence of spiritual life. One of the motivating factors for wanting to please Him is knowing you will someday stand before Jesus Christ and give account of your life. The believer's sins won't be judged because Christ already washed them away with His blood. Rather, Christ will reveal whether the believer's works were good or useless. Effectiveness, dedication, devotion, service, and usefulness will be accounted for in Christ's presence. At that time the believer will know to what degree he or she pleased Christ.

   My grandfather wrote some words in his Bible that I memorized many years ago:

   "When I stand at the judgment seat of Christ and He shows His plan for me, the plan of my life as it might have been, and I see how I blocked Him here and checked Him there and would not yield my will, will there be grief in my Savior's eyes, grief though He loves me still? He would have me rich, yet I stand there poor, stripped of all but His grace while memory runs like a hunted thing down a path I can't retrace. And then my desolate heart may well nigh break with tears I cannot shed. I will cover my face with my empty hands. I will bow my un-crowned head. O Lord, of the years that are left to me, I give them to Thy hand. Take me and break me and mold me to the pattern that Thou hast planned." No believer who desires to please Christ and lives in light of His imminent return will want to be empty-handed at the judgment.

2. 2 Peter 3:14, 18—"Since you look for these things, be diligent to be found by Him in peace, spotless and blameless. . . . Grow in the grace and knowledge of our Lord and Savior Jesus Christ."

As a thief comes unannounced, so Christ's coming will be unannounced (2 Pet. 3:10). A believer is "looking for and hastening the coming of the day of God" (v. 12). Wanting to live in blissful perfection, the believer hopes that coming is soon. When it does happen, we who know Christ will dwell in a sin-free environment in "new heavens and a new earth" (v. 13). In anticipation of that day, a believer desires to live in holiness by cultivating his relationship with Christ.

3. 1 John 3:2-3—"We are children of God, and it has not appeared as yet what we shall be. We know that, when He appears, we shall be like Him, because we shall see Him just as He is. And everyone who has this hope fixed on Him purifies himself, just as He is pure." Every believer should long to be like Christ. That was Paul's yearning when he said, "I press on toward the goal for the prize of the upward call of God in Christ Jesus" (Phil. 3:14). Knowing we will face Christ instills a desire for purity.

4. 1 John 2:28—"Abide in Him, so that when He appears, we may have confidence and not shrink away from Him in shame at His coming." A believer wants to meet Christ with joyful assurance, not with

regret like an unbeliever. To do so he must live in holiness, expecting the Lord's return at any moment. Paul said a divine reward awaits those who anticipate our Lord's return that way (2 Tim. 4:8).

Conclusion

Jesus said, "Be dressed in readiness, and keep your lamps alight. And be like men who are waiting for their master when he returns from the wedding feast, so that they may immediately open the door to him when he comes and knocks. Blessed are those slaves whom the master shall find on the alert when he comes; truly I say to you, that he will gird himself to serve, and have them recline at the table, and will come up and wait on them" (Luke 12:35-37). When Christ comes, He will serve those who waited for Him.

However, Jesus warned, "Be on the alert, for you do not know which day your Lord is coming. But be sure of this, that if the head of the house had known at what time of the night the thief was coming, he would have been on the alert and would not have allowed his house to be broken into. For this reason you be ready too; for the Son of Man is coming at an hour when you do not think He will" (Matt. 24:42-44). Christ's words are a warning not only to the lost but also to believers. We too must be ready because we don't know the moment of Christ's coming. And that's an incentive for holy living!

Focusing on the Facts

1. What characterizes the church's present spiritual condition (see pp. 20-21)?
2. What should be the basis of the believer's faith, the object of his affection, and the goal of his life (see p. 22)?
3. What are some motivating factors to help a believer be faithful in suffering (see p. 22)?
4. What does "the end of all things" refer to in 1 Peter 4:7 (see pp. 22-23)?
5. What does "is at hand" speak of in 1 Peter 4:7 (see p. 23)?

6. How should waiting for the Lord's return affect a believer's thinking (see p. 23)?

7. How could knowing the time of the Lord's return affect a believer's conduct (see pp. 23-24)?

8. James encouraged suffering believers to wait _____ for the Lord's return (James 5:7-8; see p. 25).

9. What motivates believers to gather together for worship (Heb. 10:25; see pp. 25-26)?

10. How do we know the early church was already in the last days? Support your answer with Scripture (see p. 26).

11. Explain how 2 Corinthians 5:9-10 should motivate a Christian to please Christ (see p. 28).

12. What was Paul's goal in life (Phil. 3:14)? What will that goal instill in a believer (1 John 3:2-3; see p. 29)?

13. What awaits a believer who lives to please himself (1 John 2:28; see pp. 29-30)?

14. Those who look for the Lord's return and live to please Him can expect a _____ _____ (2 Tim. 4:8; see p. 30).

15. What is Christ's attitude toward those who look for His return (Luke 12:35-37; see p. 30)?

16. Summarize the meaning of Christ's warning in Matthew 24:42-44 (see p. 30).

Pondering the Principles

1. Christ's first coming provided salvation through His death on the cross. Puritan Thomas Boston depicted Christ's presenting a sinner to the Father in this way: "Father, here is a poor creature that was born in sin, and hath lived in rebellion all his days; he hath broken all thy laws, and deserves all thy wrath; yet he is one of that number that thou gavest me before the world began; and I have made full payment to thy justice by my blood for all his debt; and now I have opened his eyes to see the sinfulness and misery of his condition: I have broken his heart for his rebellions against thee, and bowed his will into obedience to the offer of thy grace: I have united him to me by faith. . . . Since he is mine by regeneration, let him also become thine. . . . Since thy justice is satisfied for his sins, let thine anger also be turned away, and receive him graciously into favour" (*The Beauties of Boston*, Samuel M'Millan, ed. [Inverness: Christian Focus, 1979], p. 205). Has Christ forgiven

your sins so that you can anticipate His second coming with delight? If you are a believer, read 1 Peter 1:3-5, and offer thanksgiving to the Lord for His saving work through Christ's "precious blood" (v. 19).

2. Paul's ambition was to please Christ through holy living (2 Cor. 5:9-10). J. C. Ryle said, "A holy man will follow after spiritual-mindedness. He will endeavour to set his affections entirely on things above, and to hold things on earth with a very loose hand. He will not neglect the business of the life that now is; but the first place in his mind and thoughts will be given to the life to come. He will aim to live like one whose treasure is in heaven, and to pass through this world like a stranger and pilgrim travelling to his home" (*Holiness*, [Hertfordshire: Evangelical Press, 1987], p. 37). Ask the Lord to help you look for His coming so that "you seek first His kingdom and righteousness" (Matt. 6:33).

3

The Christian's Duty in a Hostile World—Part 2

Outline

Introduction
A. The Cost of Discipleship
B. The Ease of Discipleship
C. The Manifestation of Discipleship
    1. A desire to do right
    2. The discipline to do right

Review
I. The Incentive (v. 7a)

Lesson
II. The Instructions (v. 7b-11a)
A. About Personal Holiness (v. 7b)
    1. It involves godly thinking
    2. It involves spiritual alertness
    3. It involves prayerful communion
B. About Mutual Love (vv. 8-9)
    1. How we should love (v. 8a)
    2. Why we should love (v. 8b)
    3. Who we should love (v. 9)

Introduction

A. The Cost of Discipleship

1. Luke 14:26-33—Jesus said, "If anyone comes to Me, and does not hate his own father and mother and wife and children and brothers and sisters, yes, and even his own life, he cannot be My disciple. Whoever does not carry his own cross and come after Me cannot be My disciple. For which one of you, when he wants to build a tower, does not first sit down and calculate the cost, to see if he has enough to complete it? Otherwise, when he has laid a foundation, and is not able to finish, all who observe it begin to ridicule him, saying, 'This man began to build and was not able to finish.' Or what king, when he sets out to meet another king in battle, will not first sit down and take counsel whether he is strong enough with ten thousand men to encounter the one coming against him with twenty thousand? Or else, while the other is still far away, he sends a delegation and asks terms of peace. So therefore, no one of you can be My disciple who does not give up all his own possessions."

   No one should become a follower of Jesus Christ without first counting the high cost of doing so. Being an authentic Christian demands a willingness to pay the price. We need to encourage people to consider what Christ asks of them since it is costly.

2. Matthew 13:44-46—"The kingdom of heaven is like a treasure hidden in the field, which a man found and hid; and from joy over it he goes and sells all that he has, and buys that field. Again, the kingdom of heaven is like a merchant seeking fine pearls, and upon finding one pearl of great value, he went and sold all that he had, and bought it." Those parables imply that discipleship involves a commitment to Christ, which is a reflection of salvation's infinite worth.

3. Matthew 19:21—Jesus said, "If you wish to be complete, go and sell your possessions and give to the poor, and you shall have treasure in heaven; and come, follow Me." Selling material belongings and helping the poor don't merit salvation by themselves but are evidence of an obedient attitude toward Christ. Following Christ involves a willingness to do whatever He asks.

4. Luke 9:59-62—Jesus said to a man, " 'Follow Me.' But he said, 'Permit me first to go and bury my father.' But [Christ] said to him, 'Allow the dead to bury their own dead; but as for you, go and proclaim everywhere the kingdom of God.' And another also said, 'I will follow You, Lord; but first permit me to say good-bye to those at home.' But Jesus said to him, 'No one, after putting his hand to the plow and looking back, is fit for the kingdom of God.' " Nothing should interfere with following Christ.

B. The Ease of Discipleship

1. Matthew 11:29-30—Jesus said, "Take My yoke upon you. . . . For My yoke is easy, and My load is light." That's a gracious invitation, but it is still a call to submit to Christ. Discipleship is costly, but the cost of hell is greater. Proverbs 13:15 says, "The way of the treacherous is hard." To reject Christ is to choose the harder, more costly way. It is a life of crushing guilt, hopeless disappointment, unsolvable problems, and eternal condemnation in hell. The cost of following Christ is small in comparison. Discipleship is a paradox since following Jesus Christ is costly but easy.

2. 1 John 5:3—The apostle John said, "This is the love of God, that we keep His commandments; and His commandments are not burdensome." A disciple is not only called to obey His commands but also enabled by the Spirit's power to fulfill those commands. Obedience to God's Word in the Spirit's

power brings joy to the disciple because of Christ's great grace.

Because the world is complex, contemporary Christianity seems to assume that solutions to a Christian's problems are also complex. But that isn't true because God chooses common, humble people to know the things of God (1 Cor. 1:27-28). The foundations of the Christian life are simple and direct. And 1 Peter 4:7-11 supplies us with those simple, foundational elements of Christian living.

C. The Manifestation of Discipleship

1. A desire to do right

Because of the new nature implanted within his heart, a believer longs to be what God wants him to be. The apostle Paul saw sin as something he occasionally did but did not wish to do (Rom. 7:19). Although Paul wanted to obey God's law, which is holy, just, and good, he sometimes gave in to the flesh. Sin can cloud a believer's longing to do right, but his basic impulse is to hate sin and love righteousness.

2. The discipline to do right

The mere desire to do right doesn't guarantee that the believer will do that. A child's desire to be like someone else illustrates the point. Maybe a child has dreams of being a major-league baseball player. So he holds the bat the same way that his favorite player does. Or maybe he wants to be a medical doctor like his uncle. So he drapes a toy stethoscope around his neck and parades around the house. But a child doesn't become a professional baseball player or doctor through desire alone.

Fulfillment of a desire begins with a person's ability, which is developed through years of preparation. An individual needs to spend his time and energy building a foundation of habits, responses, strengths, timing, and even a memory to bring a desire to fruition. A successful moment at bat in the World Series is the result of years of disciplined preparation, not just a strong wish. Disciplined study and practice prepare a doctor for performing surgery, not merely his desire to be a surgeon.

Many Christians desire spiritual excellence because they see Christ's image in the Bible, but they fail to exercise the daily discipline required to produce that excellence. That is why some Christians fall apart in a crisis. As the crisis descends, they want to find a shortcut for spiritual strength instead of practicing the spiritual discipline of obeying God's Word. Obedience to revealed principles in His Word is the only way to be ready for a crisis. The day-to-day spiritual disciplines build the strength, courage, boldness, and depth that help a Christian be effective during his trial.

A Christian who lives in disobedience can't suddenly take control his life and instantaneously live and react the way Christ would. That would be a shallow type of Christianity. In his book *The Spirit of the Disciplines* Dallas Willard says, "The 'on-the-spot' episodes are not the place where we can, even by the grace of God, redirect unchristlike but ingrained tendencies of action toward sudden Christlikeness. Our efforts to take control at that moment will fail so uniformly and so ingloriously that the whole project of following Christ will appear ridiculous to the watching world. . . .

"Some decades ago there appeared a very successful Christian novel called *In His Steps*. The plot tells of a chain of tragic events that brings the minister of a prosperous church to realize how unlike Christ's life his own life had become. The minister then leads his congregation in a vow not to do anything without first asking themselves the question, 'What would Jesus do in this case?' As the content of the book makes clear, the author took this vow to be the same thing as intending to follow Jesus—to walk precisely

37

'in his steps.' It is, of course, a novel, but even in real life we would count on significant changes in the lives of earnest Christians who took such a vow—just as it happens in that book.

"But there is a flaw in this thinking. . . . Asking ourselves 'What would Jesus do?' when suddenly in the face of an important situation simply is not an adequate discipline or preparation to enable one to live as he lived. It no doubt will do some good and is certainly better than nothing at all, but that act alone is not sufficient to see us boldly and confidently through a crisis, and we could easily find ourselves driven to despair over the powerless tension it will put us through" ([San Francisco: Harper and Row, 1988], pp. 7-9).

Being like Jesus Christ is the result of daily spiritual discipline. And the secret of handling a crisis is learning how to live the Christian life on a day-to-day basis by developing the necessary habits, godly faith, and spiritual courage. Jesus said, "A pupil is not above his teacher; but everyone, after he has been fully trained, will be like his teacher" (Luke 6:40).

Novelist Leo Tolstoy wrote, "Man's whole life is a continual contradiction of what he knows to be his duty. In every department of life he acts in defiant opposition to the dictates of his conscience and his common sense" (cited by Dallas Willard, "Discipleship: For Christians Only?" *Christianity Today* [10 Oct. 1980]: 27). Fallen man can't even do what he thinks is right because his nature is depraved. But because of his regenerate life, a Christian can overcome that impact of fallenness by cultivating godly habits. And 1 Peter 4:7-11 instructs us of our duty to build godly habits that help us stand in the midst of hostility and whatever else we have to endure in life.

I. THE INCENTIVE (v. 7a; see pp. 22-30)

Lesson

II. THE INSTRUCTIONS (v. 7b-11a)

"Be of sound judgment and sober spirit for the purpose of prayer. Above all, keep fervent in your love for one another, because love covers a multitude of sins. Be hospitable to one another without complaint. As each one has received a special gift, employ it in serving one another, as good stewards of the manifold grace of God. Whoever speaks, let him speak, as it were, the utterances of God; whoever serves, let him do so as by the strength which God supplies."

That passage talks about holiness, love, and service. We're to concentrate our Christian living in those three dimensions. Holiness refers to our relationship to God and His revealed Word. Love affects our relationships with others. And service is our responsibility to minister within the Body of Christ.

A. About Personal Holiness (v. 7b)

"Be of sound judgment and sober spirit for the purpose of prayer."

Peter wanted every believer to be godly and pure so they could enjoy unhindered communion with God.

1. It involves godly thinking

The Greek term translated "be of sound judgment" (Gk., sōphronēsate) comes from two words that mean "to keep safe" and "the mind." It refers to guarding your mind and keeping it clear. The mind is to be fixed on spiritual priorities and holy living. The apostle

Paul said, "Set your mind on the things above, not on the things that are on earth" (Col. 3:2).

The verb also could imply not being swept away by emotion or passion. It was used to describe the maniac Jesus delivered from the legion of demons, who then was "in his right mind" (Mark 5:15).

The apostle Paul said we're not to think highly of ourselves "but to think so as to have sound judgment" (Rom. 12:3). It's important to guard your mind because a person acts according to the way he or she thinks (Prov. 23:7). Since the world is self-indulgent, deceptive, and influenced by demons, a believer can easily lose his spiritual and mental balance. Therefore a believer's focus should be on God and thoughts that please Him.

a) Joshua 1:8—The Lord said, "This book of the law shall not depart from your mouth, but you shall meditate on it day and night, so that you may be careful to do according to all that is written in it; for then you will make your way prosperous, and then you will have success." God was pointing out the importance of thinking about His Word.

b) Philippians 4:8—"Whatever is true, whatever is honorable, whatever is right, whatever is pure, whatever is lovely, whatever is of good repute, if there is any excellence and if anything worthy of praise, let your mind dwell on these things." Guarding the mind by right thinking is vital to Christian holiness.

c) Colossians 3:16—"Let the word of Christ richly dwell within you, with all wisdom teaching and admonishing one another with psalms and hymns and spiritual songs, singing with thankfulness in your hearts to God." A believer is to saturate his mind with God's Word so his thinking will be pure.

d) Titus 2:11-12—"The grace of God has appeared, bringing salvation to all men, instructing us to deny ungodliness and worldly desires and to live sensibly, righteously and godly in the present age."

Bringing the mind captive to Christ (2 Cor. 10:5) and His Word guards the mind and allows a believer to see things from an eternal perspective. That's the only way a believer can determine what's important and what's not. Sudden emotion, changing fancies, unbalanced fanaticism, or foolish indifference won't sweep away the believer who guards his mind. Rather, his thinking will be poised and balanced.

2. It involves spiritual alertness

"Sober spirit" is close in meaning to sound judgment. This term speaks of taking things seriously and being alert. Elsewhere the term is translated "be on the alert" (Matt. 24:42) and "keep watching" (Matt. 26:41).

3. It involves prayerful communion

Godly thinking ("sound judgment") and spiritual alertness ("sober spirit") are necessary "for the purpose of prayer" (1 Pet. 4:7). Cluttered, imbalanced, confused, or self-centered thinking hinders prayerful communion with God. A believer can't know the fullness of that communion if his mind is unstable due to worldly pursuits, ignorance of God's truth, or indifference to God's purposes. Attitudes determine your relationship to God and are the result of your thinking patterns. To commune with God effectively and deeply requires that you think biblically.

Unending communion with God that is born out of thinking His thoughts is the heart of a believer's life and power. A believer who deeply studies the Word in search of great truths about God experiences communion with Him that's difficult to explain because he is touching the mind of God, if ever so lightly. Even in unspoken communion, there is an overwhelming sense of His presence. That communion comes only when you are making sound judgments and are alert to divine truth.

The summation of Christian living is thinking God's thoughts. That means a believer is to read, meditate, think, and absorb God's Word daily so that his involuntary responses are godly. Out of that time in God's Word comes sweet communion, effective prayer, and spiritual power.

B. About Mutual Love (vv. 8-9)

"Above all, keep fervent in your love for one another, because love covers a multitude of sins. Be hospitable to one another without complaint."

Peter turns from the vertical aspect of holiness before God to the horizontal aspect of love toward others. That primarily refers to our relationships with other Christians but also has to do with evangelism. As Jesus said, "By this all men will know that you are My disciples, if you have love for one another" (John 13:35). Love is the substance of our witness to the world.

"Above all" speaks of the importance of love in our relationships. After a believer has strengthened his relationship with the Lord through intense Bible study and prayer, he will think with a biblical mind and a spiritual attitude. That will prepare him for any crisis. His next concern should be with loving those around him.

1. How we should love (v. 8a)

"Keep fervent in your love for one another."

Peter's instruction here is similar to what Paul said elsewhere: "Beyond all these things put on love, which is the perfect bond of unity" (Col. 3:14) and "[maintain] the same love" (Phil. 2:2). In 1 Peter 4:8 the participle translated "keep" amplifies the verbs of verse 7, which means a fervent love flows out of a balanced mind and spirit. "Fervent" refers to stretching or straining and pictures a person running with taut muscles to achieve the maximum output. Extrabiblical literature uses the term to describe a horse straining to run at full speed. So it means intensity and exertion.

Such love is sacrificial, not sentimental. By loving the unlovely and one's enemies when it doesn't seem rational and to the point where it's costly, the believer crosses the barriers of human emotion. This kind of love requires stretching all your spiritual muscles in spite of insult, injury, and misjudgment from others.

2. Why we should love (v. 8b)

"Because love covers a multitude of sins."

Criticizing each other because of our sins causes strife and divisions. Even Christians are still prone to sin occasionally because of the fallen human flesh in which we all dwell. So the only thing that will maintain our unity is love because love forgives.

Thinking he was spiritually mature and more magnanimous than anyone else, Peter said to the Lord, "How often shall my brother sin against me and I forgive him? Up to seven times?" (Matt. 18:21). Undoubtedly Peter commended himself because rabbinical teaching at that time said a person should forgive three times. But the Lord told Peter he should forgive "up to seventy times seven" (v. 22).

First Peter 4:8 is reminiscent of Proverbs 10:12: "Hatred stirs up strife, but love covers all transgressions." In 1 Peter the present tense of the verb "covers" indicates a self-evident truth: By its nature love tends to forgive a multitude of sins. God Himself is the perfect example of One who forgives. He is "rich in mercy, because of His great love with which He loved us" (Eph. 2:4).

Commentators differ on the interpretation of "love covers a multitude of sins" (1 Pet. 4:8). Some say it is God's love that covers the sins, but others say it's the love of believers who are covering each other's sins out of their love for one another. I believe the verse is an axiom. Because it's self-evident that love covers sin, the love is from God to man as well as from Christian to Christian.

The Greek term for "love" (Gk., *agapē*) carries a volitional and spiritual meaning. Our salvation is a result of God's choosing to love us (John 3:16; 1 John 4:19). "God demonstrates His own love toward us, in that while we were yet sinners, Christ died for us" (Rom. 5:8). We're to follow His lead and demonstrate our love for Him and for others. After all, that is what "the whole Law and the Prophets" depend on (Matt. 22:40). Hatred, selfishness, and self-centeredness stir up strife, but love forgives. The church would be transformed if it were to love that way. Love should be at the base of all our spiritual relationships.

3. Who we should love (v. 9)

"Be hospitable to one another without complaint."

"Be hospitable" means we should love strangers— believers we don't know. It's easier to love our friends and cover their sins, but Peter says to extend that same love to believers we don't know well. That refers not only to a spiritual love that forgives sin but also to an affectionate love that prompts you to open your heart and home to those in need. Love is intensely practical, not just an emotional feeling. In New Testament times Christians obliged to travel often couldn't stay at the inns because they tended to be houses of ill repute. Without the hospitality offered by the early church, many Christians would have found it difficult to survive.

Hebrews 13:2 says, "Do not neglect to show hospitality to strangers, for by this some have entertained

44

angels without knowing it." That is reminiscent of the time when the Lord and two of His angels visited Abraham and Sarah (Gen. 18:1-2). And according to the law, the Jewish people were to extend hospitality to strangers (Ex. 22:21; Deut. 14:29). Jesus commended believers for providing food, clothing, and shelter for others (Matt. 25:35-40). And He taught that we should invite the poor, the blind, and the lame into our homes and feed them (Luke 14:12-14). God honors those kinds of sacrifices for others.

The spirit of hospitality is more than providing a meal and opening a door. Being hospitable involves loving people outside our normal circle and doing it without grumbling. Hospitality doesn't mean the "Poor Richard's Almanac mentality," which says that fish and visitors smell in three days! Rather, we're to open our hearts to those we don't know.

Focusing on the Facts

1. In what sense is discipleship costly? Support your answer with Scripture (see pp. 34-35).
2. In what sense is discipleship easy? Support your answer with Scripture (see pp. 35-36).
3. What does Romans 7:19 teach us about discipleship (see p. 36)?
4. How can a Christian be prepared to handle a crisis (see p. 37)?
5. What does "be of sound judgment" (1 Pet. 4:7) mean? Support your answer with Scripture (see pp. 39-40).
6. What Scriptures show that a believer's focus should be on God and His Word (see pp. 40-41)?
7. What does "sober spirit" mean in 1 Peter 4:7 (see p. 41)?
8. How do sound judgment and a sober spirit relate to prayer (1 Pet. 4:7; see p. 41)?
9. How does a believer have prayerful communion with God (see pp. 41-42)?
10. The summation of Christian living is _____ _____ _____ (see p. 42).
11. What is the significance of "keep" in 1 Peter 4:8 (see p. 43)?

12. Explain the meaning of "fervent" in 1 Peter 4:8 (see p. 43).
13. In what sense is love sacrificial (see p. 43)?
14. What lesson did the Lord teach Peter about forgiveness (Matt. 18:21; see p. 43)?
15. Whose love is covering the sins in 1 Peter 4:8 (see p. 43)?
16. What does "be hospitable" (1 Pet. 4:9) mean? Support your answer with Scripture (see pp. 44-45).

Pondering the Principles

1. First Peter 4:7 instructs us of our duty concerning personal holiness. J. C. Ryle said, "Holiness is the habit of being of one mind with God, according as we find His mind described in Scripture. It is the habit of agreeing in God's judgement, hating what He hates, loving what He loves, and measuring everything in this world by the standard of His Word. He who most entirely agrees with God, he is the most holy man" (*Holiness* [Hertfordshire: Evangelical Press, 1987], p. 34). It is important for you to regularly study God's Word so you can be of one mind with God. Sound judgment and spiritual alertness are the fruition of deeply studying His Word. Plan to begin studying Scripture. If you already are, be encouraged to continue so that you will be "approved to God as a workman who does not need to be ashamed, handling accurately the word of truth" (2 Tim. 2:15).

2. A believer who loves fervently readily forgives the sins of others. Author Jerry Bridges said, "Forgiveness cost God his Son on the cross, but what does it cost us to forgive one another? Forgiving costs us our sense of justice. We all have this innate sense deep within our souls, but it has been perverted by our selfish sinful natures. We want to see 'justice' done, but the justice we envision satisfies our own interests. We must realize that justice has been done. God is the only rightful administrator of justice in all of creation, and his justice has been satisfied. In order to forgive our brother, we must be satisfied with God's justice and forego the satisfaction of our own" (*The Practice of Godliness* [Colorado Springs: Navpress, 1983], p. 252). Read Ephesians 4:32 and Colossians 3:13, and ask the Lord to help you have a fervent love that forgives others.

4

The Christian's Duty in a Hostile World—Part 3

Outline

Introduction
A. Salvation Is a New Life
B. Salvation Results in Good Works

Review
I.   The Incentive (v. 7a)
II. The Instructions (vv. 7b-11a)
     A. Concerning Personal Holiness (v. 7b)
     B. Concerning Mutual Love (vv. 8-9)

Lesson
     C. Concerning Spiritual Service (vv. 10-11a)
        1. The extent of spiritual gifts (v. 10a)
           a) An explanation
           b) An illustration
        2. The source of spiritual gifts (v. 10b)
        3. The use of spiritual gifts (v. 10c)
           a) Everyone benefits
           b) Everyone is important
           c) Everyone is responsible
        4. The variety of spiritual gifts (v. 10d)
        5. The categories of spiritual gifts (v. 11)

Conclusion

Introduction

A. Salvation Is a New Life

Salvation is more than the forgiveness of sins. It's a transformation of a person's life. Without transformation the cross remains as the focal point of salvation. As vital as the cross is to Christianity, it wasn't the early church's central focus. Kenneth Clark in his book *Civilisation* points out that the cross was a late symbol in Christian art and culture. He determined that its first appearance as such was in A.D. 430 in the church of Santa Sabina at Rome, where it's located obscurely in a corner ([New York: Harper and Row, 1969], p. 29).

Instead the church focused on the resurrection and the believer's new life in Christ. Of course His death paid the penalty for our sins and we died in Christ spiritually, but we also arose in Christ to walk in newness of life! In salvation God "delivered us from the domain of darkness, and transferred us to the kingdom of His beloved Son" (Col. 1:13). So new life is regeneration—the imparting of divine life into man's soul.

B. Salvation Results in Good Works

Divinely implanted within each believer is a holy and incorruptible seed. That seed bears the fruit of good works, which the apostle James said are inherent in the nature of saving faith (James 2:17).

Reformer Martin Luther described saving faith this way: "O, this faith is a living, busy, active, powerful thing! It is impossible that it should not be ceaselessly doing that which is good. It does not even ask whether good works should be done; but before the question can be asked, it has done them, and it is constantly engaged in doing them. But he who does not do such works, is a man without faith. He gropes and casts about him to find faith and good works, not knowing what either of them is, and yet prattles and idly multiplies words about faith and good works. . . .

"Faith is a living, well-founded confidence in the grace of God, so perfectly certain that it would die a thousand times rather than surrender its conviction. Such confidence and personal knowledge of divine grace makes its possessor joyful, bold, and full of warm affection toward God and all created things—all of which the Holy Spirit works in faith. Hence, such a man becomes without constraint willing and eager to do good to everyone, to serve everyone, to suffer all manner of ills, in order to please and glorify God, who has shown toward him such grace" (cited by Harry Emerson Fosdick, *Great Voices of the Reformation* [New York: Random House, 1952], pp. 121-22).

Because the impulse to obey God's Word is inherent in our new life, it's only natural that Jesus would say part of the Great Commission is "teaching them to observe all that I commanded you" (Matt. 28:20). First Peter 4:7-11 draws on that impulse by telling us our duty in a hostile world.

Review

I.   THE INCENTIVE (v. 7*a*; see pp. 22-30)

II. THE INSTRUCTIONS (vv. 7*b*-11*a*)

A. About Personal Holiness (v. 7*b*; see pp. 39-42)

B. About Mutual Love (vv. 8-9; see pp. 42-44)

Lesson

C. Concerning Spiritual Service (vv. 10-11*a*)

"As each one has received a special gift, employ it in serving one another, as good stewards of the manifold grace of God. Whoever speaks, let him speak, as it were, the utterances of God; whoever serves, let him do so as by the strength which God supplies."

Inner holiness leads to outward love, which manifests itself through spiritual service. But spiritual service without inward holiness or outward love is hypocrisy and legalism. "Serving" means "to wait on someone." It is like a table waiter who does common, ordinary tasks. We should live to serve others in practical ways, and we do that by using our spiritual gifts.

1. The extent of spiritual gifts (v. 10a)

"Each one."

a) An explanation

Every Christian has a special gift. The apostle Paul said, "To each one is given the manifestation of the Spirit for the common good. . . . The same Spirit works all these things, distributing to each one individually just as He wills" (1 Cor. 12:7, 11). As every part of a human body has a certain function, so also does each member of Christ's Body. That's because "the body is not one member, but many" (1 Cor. 12:14).

The Spirit distributes gifts "individually" (1 Cor. 12:11). That term means "peculiar to oneself" and refers to our uniqueness as spiritual snowflakes. As our fingerprints identify us in the physical realm, so our special blend of spiritual gifts marks us as unique in the spiritual realm. Therefore, the gifts are universal (every believer has one) as well as individual (each gift is uniquely given).

b) An illustration

How can the Spirit divide the few gifts listed in His Word among millions of Christians and still make each one unique? Try thinking of the gifts as colors on a palette. God dips His brush into different color or gift categories and paints each believer a unique color.

Not only does God color our gifts in different ways (Eph. 4:7), but He also gives us the right amount of faith to use them (Rom. 12:3). Paul stated it again this way: "There are varieties of gifts, but the same Spirit. And there are varieties of ministries, and the same Lord. And there are varieties of effects, but the same God who works all things in all persons" (1 Cor. 12:4-6).

2. The source of spiritual gifts (v. 10b)

"Has received a special gift."

The Spirit supernaturally gives, controls, and energizes the gifts; therefore we can't earn, pray for, or generate them. The Greek term translated "gift" in Ephesians 4:7 (Gk., dōreas) emphasizes that it's freely given, and the term in 1 Peter 4:10 (charisma) underscores the aspect of grace. Sometimes "spiritual" (Gk., pneumatikos) modifies "gift" to stress its spiritual character and capacity.

In New Testament usage charisma refers both to spiritual gifts and to salvation. Both are equally gracious because both are undeserved and unearned. A gift doesn't involve human talent but is a divine capacity to minister as part of Christ's Body.

3. The use of spiritual gifts (v. 10c)

"Employ it in serving one another, as good stewards."

a) Everyone benefits

"For the common good" (1 Cor. 12:7) indicates that every gift mutually benefits Christ's Body. Conversely, non-use adversely affects it. As Paul said, "If the foot should say, 'Because I am not a hand, I am not a part of the body,' it is not for this reason any the less a part of the body. And if the ear should say, 'Because I am not an eye, I am not a part of the body,' it is not for this reason any the less a part of the body. If the whole body were an eye, where would the hearing be? If the whole were hearing, where would the sense of smell be? But now God has placed the members, each one of them, in the body, just as He desired. And if they were all one member, where would the body be? But now there are many members, but one body. And the eye cannot say to the hand, 'I have no need of you'; or again the head to the feet, 'I have no need of you.' On the contrary, it is much truer that the members of the body which seem to be weaker are necessary" (vv. 15-22).

b) Everyone is important

Sometimes we wrongly depreciate members of Christ's Body: "Those members of the body, which we deem less honorable, on these we bestow more abundant honor, and our unseemly members come to have more abundant seemliness, whereas our seemly members have no need of it. But God has so composed the body, giving more abundant honor to that member which lacked, that there should be no division in the body, but that the members should have the same care for one another" (vv. 23-25).

The visible, outwardly prolific members aren't necessarily the most important ones. Rather, we're to value every believer's role. And a believer who says, "I'll only serve if I'm a hand or an eye," is being disobedient to God's Word. That's because we're saved to serve.

c) Everyone is responsible

"Good stewards" (1 Pet. 4:10) tells us we're to be responsible in managing our gifts. In Bible times, a steward handled an owner's land, funds, food supplies, and other resources. Today we must properly use the gifts that God gives us. Not serving others with your gifts hurts the Body's health since no believer can take your place.

4. The variety of spiritual gifts (v. 10*d*)

    "Of the manifold grace of God."

    "Manifold" means "many-colored," referring to multi-faceted giftedness. Two believers can have a gift of teaching but each with a unique blend of grace and faith. That provides great diversity in the Body of Christ! Someone may preach with an emphasis on showing mercy, and another may preach with an emphasis on discerning the truth. So the use of a gift varies from person to person.

    We're better off not trying to identify our gifts in a technical way. A computer study can't identify our gifts. Rather, our service in the church under the Spirit's control is our gift. And that kind of service produces a positive impact. Although we won't be able to precisely identify our gifts, we can observe how the Spirit uses us when we're available to Him.

5. The categories of spiritual gifts (v. 11)

    "Whoever speaks, let him speak, as it were, the utterances of God; whoever serves, let him do so as by the strength which God supplies."

    A believer has either a speaking or serving gift. Speaking gifts include preaching, teaching, wisdom, knowledge, discernment, or leadership. To others He gives serving gifts such as administration, prayer, showing mercy, or helps.

    If a believer has a speaking gift, he's to communicate "the utterances of God"—a reference to Scripture (Acts 7:38; Rom. 3:2). A serving gift is to be done "by the strength which God supplies."

Conclusion

Why are we to do all that? "So that in all things God may be glorified through Jesus Christ, to whom belongs the glory and dominion forever and ever. Amen" (1 Pet. 4:11). The purpose of our holiness, love, and service is to glorify God. "In all things" refers to all matters of Christian duty. This is a doxology—a word about praise or glory. We can only glorify God "through Jesus Christ." Commentators have long discussed whether "to whom" refers to God or Jesus Christ. It is a blessed and inspired ambiguity because the glory belongs to God in Christ and Christ in God.

The apostle Paul said, "Whether, then, you eat or drink or whatever you do, do all to the glory of God" (1 Cor. 10:31). A Christian should want to glorify God in everything. The way to do that is to live in light of the second coming of Christ (1 Pet. 4:7a) and fulfill our obligations of holiness, love, and service (vv. 7b-11). Peter couldn't resist saying "amen" to conclude the matter. It means "so let it be." Along with Peter we should say, "Let my life be for the glory of God!"

Focusing on the Facts

1. How did the early church view salvation (see p. 48)?
2. _____ _____ are inherent in the nature of saving faith (James 2:17; see p. 48).
3. How did Martin Luther describe saving faith (see pp. 48-49)?
4. Inner _____ leads to outward _____ , which manifests itself through spiritual _____ (see p. 50).
5. Explain and illustrate the extent of spiritual gifts (see pp. 50-51).
6. Name the source of spiritual gifts (see p. 51).
7. Explain the similarity between spiritual gifts and salvation (see p. 51).
8. In 1 Corinthians 12:7 what does "for the common good" refer to? How do the following verses illustrate that point (see pp. 51-52)?
9. What does "good stewards" tell us in 1 Peter 4:10 (see pp. 52-53)?

10. Explain the meaning of "manifold" in 1 Peter 4:10 (see p. 53).
11. Is it necessary to identify your gift? Explain (see p. 53).
12. What are the two categories of gifts (1 Pet. 4:11; see p. 53)?
13. Explain the relation of "utterances" in 1 Peter 4:11 to the use of gifts (Acts 7:38; Rom. 3:2; see p. 53).
14. What should be the goal of everything you do (1 Cor. 10:31; 1 Pet. 4:11; see p. 54)?

Pondering the Principles

1. The gift of helps (1 Cor. 12:28) is a vital ministry. Maybe you can't teach, preach, or sing well, but perhaps you can help clean a house, prepare a meal, mow the lawn, or make household or mechanical repairs for a needy believer. Don't overlook the significance of deeds that appear to be common and ordinary since they're all essential to the health of the Body of Christ.

2. We've learned that the purpose of spiritual gifts is for "serving one another" (1 Pet. 4:10). Christ is the perfect example of a servant. At the Last Supper He washed His disciples' feet and said, "If I then, the Lord and the Teacher, washed your feet, you also ought to wash one another's feet. For I gave you an example that you also should do as I did to you" (John 13:14-15). He also said, "Whoever wishes to become great among you shall be your servant, and whoever wishes to be first among you shall be your slave; just as the Son of Man did not come to be served, but to serve" (Matt. 20:26-28). Are you using your gift to serve others in the church?

5

The Fiery Trial—Part 1

Outline

Introduction
A. The Destruction of Rome
B. The Persecution of Christians

Lesson
I.   Expect Suffering (v. 12)
     A. It's the Price of Discipleship
        1. Disciples need the assurance of God's love
        2. Disciples face many difficulties in life
     B. It's a Test of Genuine Faith
II. Rejoice in Suffering (vv. 13-14)
     A. Our Attitude
     B. Our Motivation
        1. The sufferings of Christ (v. 13a)
        2. The return of Christ (v. 13b)
        3. The name of Christ (v. 14)
           a) It's the cause of reproach
           b) It's the source of blessing
              (1) Because of the Spirit's presence
              (2) Because of the Spirit's power

Introduction

A. The Destruction of Rome

On July 19, A.D. 64, during the reign of Emperor Nero, the city of Rome was consumed in a holocaust of fire. It was a city of narrow streets and high, wooden tenements that were built close together. The fire spread rapidly and lasted three days and nights. The Roman populace believed that Nero was responsible for burning their great city because he had a strange fixation for building a new city. As the city burned to the ground, he watched gleefully from the Tower of Maecenas. His soldiers not only hindered people who tried to extinguish the fire but also started new fires. The destruction devastated the Roman people because they lost everything—their religious temples, their household gods, their homes. Obviously their resentment was great. Needing to divert the attention away from himself, Nero chose the Christians as his scapegoat. Publicly he blamed them for burning Rome.

It was a crafty choice because Christians were already the innocent victims of hatred and slander. False rumors spread that they ate human flesh and drank blood during Communion and that the holy kiss was in fact unbridled lust. Furthermore, the Romans associated them with the Jewish people. Since hatred for the Jewish populace was growing at the time, it was easy to have an anti-Christian attitude as well. The Christian faith was also unpopular because there was tension in the family structure when one spouse became a believer but the other did not.

B. The Persecution of Christians

That initial hatred against the Christians eventually turned into a fixed policy of persecution under various Roman emperors. Honest judges who were prepared to acquit believers of the unfounded charges were overpowered and ignored. Instead, the false charge of anarchy against a civilized society stood against them. As a result, Christians were used as human torches to light Nero's garden parties, sewn inside wild animal skins for hunting dogs to devour, nailed to crosses, and subjected to other atrocious acts.

Many believers perished in that delirium of savagery. H. B. Workman in his book *Persecution in the Early Church* says, "For two hundred years [from Nero on] the leaders among the Christians were branded as 'anarchists' and 'atheists,' and hated accordingly. . . . To become a Christian meant the great renunciation, the joining of a despised and persecuted sect, the swimming against the tide of popular prejudice, the coming under the ban of the Empire, the possibility at any moment of imprisonment and death under its most fearful forms. . . . He that would follow Christ must count the cost, and be prepared to pay the same with his liberty and life. . . . The mere profession of Christianity was itself a crime. *Christianus sum* [I am a Christian] was almost the one plea for which there was no forgiveness, in itself all that was necessary as a 'title' on the back of the condemned. . . . For [many] the Name itself . . . meant the rack, the blazing shirt of pitch, the lion, the panther, or in the case of maidens an infamy worse than death" ([Cincinnati: Jennings and Graham, n.d.], pp. 103-4).

First Peter was probably written just after that persecution began, toward the end of A.D. 64. Believers were experiencing a "fiery ordeal" indeed (1 Pet. 4:12). So the apostle Peter told them how to respond to suffering. In a way this letter sums up all his previous instruction about that subject.

Lesson

I. EXPECT SUFFERING (v. 12)

"Beloved, do not be surprised at the fiery ordeal among you, which comes upon you for your testing, as though some strange thing were happening to you."

Throughout his letter Peter says that persecution is inevitable. In fact, the surprise would be if it didn't come. The apostle John said, "Do not marvel, brethren, if the world hates you" (1 John 3:13); Jesus said to His disciples, "If the world hates you, you know that it has hated Me before it hated you" (John 15:18); and the apostle Paul said, "All who desire to live godly in Christ Jesus will be persecuted" (2 Tim. 3:12).

A. It's the Price of Discipleship

To the lost, proclaiming Christ's name is like the unwelcome prick of the conscience because it confronts them with their sin. That confrontation often results in suffering, which is the price of discipleship. Therefore it's necessary to consider the cost of discipleship before deciding to follow Christ. Certainly Jesus had that in mind when He observed that no one builds a tower or goes into battle without first calculating the cost (Luke 14:28-32). Taking up the cross to follow Christ means pain and perhaps even death (v. 27).

1. Disciples need the assurance of God's love

"Beloved" (1 Pet. 4:12) is a pastoral term that conveys tenderness, compassion, affection, and care. Both the "sincere love of the brethren" (1:22) and the fervent love covering a multitude of sins (4:8) are expressed in that single word. Such love is a sweet pillow for our weary souls to rest on in the midst of persecution.

Suffering can tempt us to doubt God's love. If someone like Nero rolled our children in pitch and used them as human torches, we would wonder about God's love. In the midst of such persecution the enemy might echo in our ears these vile words once uttered by Job's wife: "Do you still hold fast your integrity? Curse God and die!" (Job 2:9). So Peter wrote to assure the believers of his day—and ours—of God's unfailing love.

2. Disciples face many difficulties in life

It shouldn't shock us that life is difficult. When someone takes issue with our testimony, when employees at work are hostile toward us, or when our neighbors have a vendetta against us, it's no surprise since suffering is corollary to the Christian faith. That's because following Christ promises suffering, not immunity from it. Instead of saying Jesus wants us all to be happy, healthy, and wealthy and that He'll solve all our worldly problems, we need to say truthfully to the ungodly, "You're in desperate need of Jesus Christ because you're on your way to eternal hell. You have the choice of suffering in hell forever or suffering here for a while as a Christian."

Yet some want to live under the illusion that being a Christian and serving the church eliminates every difficulty. Rather, when God effectively uses us as we're faithful to His Word, we will arouse animosity. In the words of the apostle Paul, "We are a fragrance of Christ to God among those who are being saved and among those who are perishing; to the one an aroma from death to death, to the other an aroma from life to life" (2 Cor. 2:15-16).

B. It's a Test of Genuine Faith

The Greek term translated "fiery ordeal" speaks of burning and pictures a furnace that melts down metal to purge it of foreign elements. For example Psalm 66:10 says, "[God] hast tried us with fire as silver is tried" (Septuagint). It's symbolic of affliction, which the Lord designs for our spiritual purity. First Peter 1:6-7 says, "In [the eternal salvation yet to come] you greatly rejoice, even though now for a little while, if necessary, you have been distressed by various trials, that the proof of your faith, being more precious than gold which is perishable, even though tested by fire, may be found to result in praise and glory and honor at the revelation of Jesus Christ."

Believers are willing to endure adversity because they know it proves the genuineness of their faith, which will be rewarded at Christ's appearing. The fiery trial doesn't refer to just any trouble but to persecution for living the Christian faith.

Suffering for righteousness' sake reveals whether an individual is really a true believer. Christ illustrated that point in the parable of the soils: A sower scattered some seed on stony ground, and a plant grew quickly, but its roots didn't grow deeply since the soil was shallow. Consequently, under the punishing rays of the sun, the plant died without ever bearing fruit (Matt. 13:5-6).

Our Lord was describing a shallow response to the gospel—not allowing the Word to penetrate the depths of one's heart. Persecution revealed it to be nothing but a superficial profession (vv. 20-21). That's why the persecuted church is the pure church. Through tribulation our Lord purges and cleanses the church of its chaff.

In 1 Peter 4:12 the verb translated "were happening" indicates that this fiery affliction is by God's design, not because of chance. His design is to remove our pride and self-control that we might depend on Him.

II. REJOICE IN SUFFERING (vv. 13-14)

"To the degree that you share the sufferings of Christ, keep on rejoicing; so that also at the revelation of His glory, you may rejoice with exultation. If you are reviled for the name of Christ, you are blessed, because the Spirit of glory and of God rests upon you."

A. Our Attitude

"Keep on rejoicing" indicates the attitude we're to have in the midst of trials. Anything the world brings against us for the sake of righteousness is cause for rejoicing. Jesus emphasized that by saying, "Blessed are those who have been persecuted for the sake of righteousness, for theirs is the kingdom of heaven. Blessed are you when men cast insults at you, and persecute you, and say all kinds of evil against you falsely, on account of Me. Rejoice, and be glad, for your reward in heaven is great, for so they persecuted the prophets who were before you" (Matt. 5:10-12).

B. Our Motivation

1. The sufferings of Christ (v. 13a)

"To the degree that you share the sufferings of Christ [now]."

In suffering for what is right we are partners in the same kind of sufferings Jesus endured. Jesus Christ endured earthly sufferings at the hands of sinners because He was without sin. So we shouldn't be perplexed or discouraged when it's our privilege to share in the same kind of sufferings He experienced.

2. The return of Christ (v. 13b)

"To the degree that you share the sufferings of Christ, keep on rejoicing; so that also at the revelation of His glory, you may rejoice with exultation."

"The revelation of His glory" is "the day that the Son of Man is revealed" (Luke 17:30) and refers to Christ's second coming. Christ received that glory when He ascended to heaven, but it hasn't been revealed yet on earth for man to see. However, His glory in His second coming will be so great that everyone will see it (Matt. 24:30).

When He returns, believers will "rejoice with exultation." Peter twice uses the term "rejoice" (Gk., chairō) in this verse, but the second time it's qualified by "exultation" (Gk., agallomai), a reference to rapturous joy. The sense of the verse is, "Keep on being happy, for if you do so, some day you'll be ecstatic!" If we're faithful to Christ by sharing in His sufferings in this life, we'll experience a joy that surpasses all others when He returns.

"To the degree" indicates that our eternal reward is a direct reflection of our earthly suffering. That's because suffering reveals our faithfulness to Christ. Jesus Himself pointed out the relation between the two in saying, "Blessed are you when men hate you, and ostracize you, and cast insults at you, and spurn your name as evil, for the sake of the Son of Man. Be glad in that day, and leap for joy, for behold, your reward is great in heaven; for in the same way their fathers used to treat the prophets" (Luke 6:22-23).

3. The name of Christ (v. 14)

"If you are reviled for the name of Christ, you are blessed, because the Spirit of glory and of God rests upon you."

a) It's the cause of reproach

"Reviled" means "to heap insults upon." In the Old Testament and Septuagint it means reproach heaped on God and His people by the ungodly, and in the New Testament it refers to indignities and mistreatments against Christ—the things that He endured at the hands of sinners. Since His name sums up all that He is, "for the name of Christ" indicates that we represent all that He is. It also implies that we're publicly proclaiming His name, which is what causes the hostility. So the verse is speaking of those who are reviled for proclaiming the name of Christ. In the days of the early church, the lost would exclaim with exasperation, "Christians are always talking about that name!" (cf. Acts 4:17-18; 17:6). And if we identify with the name of Jesus Christ and tell others about Him, we'll be reproached and insulted, just as our brothers and sisters in the early church were.

"Name" became synonymous with Christ Himself. In Acts 5:41 the apostles "went on their way from the presence of the [Sanhedrin], rejoicing that they had been considered worthy to suffer shame for His name." Peter said, "There is salvation in no one else; for there is no other name under heaven that has been given among men, by which we must be saved" (4:12). When the Lord confronted the apostle Paul on the Damascus Road, He said, "I will show him how much he must suffer for My name's sake" in proclaiming the good news to the lost (9:16). Acts 15:26 says, "Men . . . risked their lives for the name of our Lord Jesus Christ."

b) It's the source of blessing

"Blessed" (1 Pet. 4:14) means "fortunate." As we just observed, we will gain an eternal weight of glory for the privilege of sharing Christ's sufferings (cf. Luke 6:22-23). We're also fortunate because "the Spirit of glory and of God rests upon [us]" (v. 14). That's a reference to the objective presence and power of the Holy Spirit, not our subjective happiness.

(1)   Because of the Spirit's presence

"Glory" refers to the Spirit's essential attribute. To many of the Jewish believers in the early church, it was a reminder of the *Shekinah*, a symbol of God's presence. At the inauguration of the Tabernacle and Temple, "the glory of the Lord [His presence or *Shekinah*] filled the house of the Lord" (1 Kings 8:11). So we are privileged to have God's presence with us when we suffer for Christ; we become like Moses, whose face was shining with the glory of God (Ex. 33:29), or like the Tabernacle, so laden with God's glory "that the priests could not stand to minister because of the cloud" (1 Kings 8:11).

(2)   Because of the Spirit's power

As the *Shekinah* rested in the Tabernacle and the Temple, the Spirit in His glorious splendor and power rested upon suffering Christians. "Rests" (1 Pet. 4:14) describes refreshment in the sense of taking over for us as the dominant power in the midst of our suffering.

That rest came upon Stephen, a deacon in the Jerusalem church. As he stood before the Sanhedrin to give a defense for his faith, the religious leaders "saw his face like the face of an angel," signifying serenity, tranquillity, and a gentle joy unaffected by hostility (Acts 6:15). The leaders became infuriated as Stephen explained the Scriptures to them, but Stephen, unaffected by it all, "gazed intently into heaven and saw the glory of God, and Jesus standing at the right hand of God; and he said, 'Behold, I see the heavens opened up and the Son of Man standing at the right hand of God'" (7:55-56).

The Spirit took control of his life, allowing him the matchless privilege of seeing Christ in His glory, and he became oblivious to all else. As his enemies stoned him to death, "he called upon the Lord and said, 'Lord Jesus, receive my spirit. . . . Do not hold this sin against them!' And having said this, he fell asleep" (7:59-60).

Reading *Foxe's Book of Martyrs*, it's natural to wonder, *How could those martyred Christians transcend such enormous physical pain? How could they be singing hymns and praising God? How could they forgive their tormentors?* The answer is they saw the richness of sharing Christ's sufferings, they knew their suffering issued an eternal weight of glory, and the Spirit of glory rested upon them, taking them beyond the physical realm.

Focusing on the Facts

1. Why did Nero blame the Christians for burning Rome (see p. 58)?
2. Describe the kind of persecution believers experienced as a result (see pp. 58-59).
3. How does the writing of 1 Peter relate to the Roman persecution (see p. 59)?
4. How did Peter assure believers that they were loved (1 Pet. 4:12; see p. 60)?
5. How does God effectively use us in trials (2 Cor. 2:15-16; see p. 61)?
6. What is the spiritual benefit of a "fiery ordeal" (1 Pet. 4:12; see pp. 61-62)?
7. What lesson did Christ teach in the parable about the stony soil (Matt. 13:5-6, 20-21; see p. 62)?
8. How should the sufferings of Christ motivate you to rejoice while enduring trials (1 Pet. 4:13; see pp. 62-63)?
9. What is the reason the believer will "rejoice with exultation" at Christ's second coming (1 Pet. 4:13; see p. 63)?
10. Suffering reveals our _____ to Christ (see p. 64).
11. In what specific way is the name of Christ the cause for reproach (1 Pet. 4:14; see p. 64)?
12. In 1 Peter 4:14 "name" is synonymous with _____ _____. Support your answer with Scripture (see pp. 64-65).
13. Whose presence supports us during trials (1 Pet. 4:14; see p. 65)?
14. Explain how the Holy Spirit's power rested upon Stephen (Acts 6:15; 7:55-56, 59-60; see p. 66).

Pondering the Principles

1. The Spirit controlled Stephen's life so that he was occupied with Christ, not his adversity (Acts 6:15; 7:55-56, 59-60). Jerry Bridges wrote, "The Christian life is intended to be one of

continuous growth. We all want to grow, but we often resist the process. This is because we tend to focus on the events of adversity themselves, rather than looking with the eye of faith beyond the events to what God is doing in our lives. It was said of Jesus that He 'for the joy set before him endured the cross, scorning its shame' (Hebrews 12:2). Christ's death on the cross with its intense physical agony and infinite spiritual suffering of bearing God's wrath for our sins was the greatest calamity to ever come upon a human being. Yet Jesus could look beyond that suffering to the joy set before Him. . . . We are to look beyond our adversity to what God is doing in our lives and rejoice in the certainty that He is at work in us to cause us to grow" (*Trusting God* [Colorado Springs: Navpress, 1988], p. 175). When you suffer for righteousness' sake, be encouraged that "the Spirit of glory and of God rests upon you" (1 Pet. 4:14). Like Moses, you can endure, "seeing Him who is unseen" (Heb. 11:27).

2. The apostle Paul said, "[Our] momentary, light affliction is producing for us an eternal weight of glory far beyond all comparison" (2 Cor. 4:17). Thomas Watson gave a similar encouragement for persevering in trials: "You are within a few days' march of heaven. Salvation is near to you. . . . Christians, it is but a while and you will have done weeping and praying, and be triumphing; you shall put off your mourning, and put on white robes; you shall put off your armour, and put on a victorious crown. You who have made a good progress in religion, you are almost ready to commence and take your degree of glory; now is your salvation nearer than when you began to believe. . . . Though the way be up-hill and full of thorns, yet you have gone the greatest part of your way, and shortly shall rest from your labours" (*A Body of Divinity* [Edinburgh: The Banner of Truth Trust, 1986], p. 286). To persevere in trials, "look not at the things which are seen, but at the things which are not seen; for the things which are seen are temporal, but the things which are not seen are eternal" (2 Cor. 4:18).

6

The Fiery Trial—Part 2

Outline

Introduction
A. Hostility Against the Early Church
B. Hostility Against Today's Church

Review
I. Expect Suffering (v. 12)
II. Rejoice in Suffering (vv. 13-14)

Lesson
III. Evaluate Your Suffering (vv. 15-18)
    A. Suffering for the Wrong Reasons (v. 15)
        1. For being a lawbreaker (v. 15a)
        2. For being a troublemaker (v. 15b)
            a) The term explained
            b) The term applied
    B. Suffering for the Right Reasons (vv. 16-18)
        1. For righteous living (v. 16)
        2. For spiritual cleansing (vv. 17-18)
            a) What it is
            b) Why it is necessary
            c) Why it is preferable
IV. Entrust Yourself to God (v. 19)
    A. An Explanation About Commitment
    B. An Example of Commitment

Introduction

A. Hostility Against the Early Church

The apostle Peter knew his readers would be experiencing the fury of anti-Christians. So throughout his letter, he expresses his concern about their suffering for righteousness.

1. 1 Peter 1:6-7—"In this you greatly rejoice, even though now for a little while, if necessary, you have been distressed by various trials, that the proof of your faith, being more precious than gold which is perishable, even though tested by fire, may be found to result in praise and glory and honor at the revelation of Jesus Christ." Trials purify our faith.

2. 1 Peter 2:11-12—Peter said, "Beloved, I urge you as aliens and strangers to abstain from fleshly lusts, which wage war against the soul. Keep your behavior excellent among the Gentiles, so that in the thing in which they slander you as evildoers, they may on account of your good deeds, as they observe them, glorify God in the day of visitation." As foreigners and pilgrims, our holy conduct is a witness to the lost and a defense against false accusations.

3. 1 Peter 2:19-20—"This finds favor, if for the sake of conscience toward God a man bears up under sorrows when suffering unjustly. For what credit is there if, when you sin and are harshly treated, you endure it with patience? But if when you do what is right and suffer for it you patiently endure it, this finds favor with God."

4. 1 Peter 3:8-9—"Let all be harmonious, sympathetic, brotherly, kindhearted, and humble in spirit; not returning evil for evil, or insult for insult, but giving a blessing instead; for you were called for the very purpose that you might inherit a blessing."

5. 1 Peter 3:14, 17—"Even if you should suffer for the sake of righteousness, you are blessed. And do not fear their intimidation, and do not be troubled. . . . For it is better, if God should will it so, that you suffer for doing what is right rather than for doing what is wrong."

6. 1 Peter 4:1—"Since Christ has suffered in the flesh, arm yourselves also with the same purpose, because he who has suffered in the flesh has ceased from sin." We should expect suffering since Christ experienced it.

7. 1 Peter 5:10—"After you have suffered for a little while, the God of all grace, who called you to His eternal glory in Christ, will Himself perfect, confirm, strengthen and establish you."

B. Hostility Against Today's Church

The church in eastern Europe has endured harsh suffering for many years, but presently it's experiencing new freedom. In some ways their freedom might be greater than ours. That's because the church there is growing stronger as it emerges from an atheistic society, but here the church faces increasing aggression from our amoral and humanistic society. Hostility against the church for speaking against the sins of our culture is already frightful and threatening. To endure the present, as well as what we might face in the future, we need to heed the teaching of 1 Peter 4:15-19, which tells us the proper way to deal with suffering for righteousness.

Review

I. EXPECT SUFFERING (v. 12; see pp. 59-62)

II. REJOICE IN SUFFERING (vv. 13-14; see pp. 62-66)

III.   EVALUATE YOUR SUFFERING (vv. 15-18)

"By no means let any of you suffer as a murderer, or thief, or evildoer, or a troublesome meddler; but if anyone suffers as a Christian, let him not feel ashamed, but in that name let him glorify God. For it is time for judgment to begin with the household of God; and if it begins with us first, what will be the outcome for those who do not obey the gospel of God? And if it is with difficulty that the righteous is saved, what will become of the godless man and the sinner?"

A. Suffering for the Wrong Reasons (v. 15)

1.   For being a lawbreaker (v. 15*a*)

"By no means let any of you suffer as a murderer, or thief, or evildoer."

If you murder someone or steal, you have no right to complain about being punished. The same is true for an "evildoer," a term that covers all the crimes not included in the first two. All those terms refer to lawbreakers.

2.   For being a troublemaker (v. 15*b*)

"Or a troublesome meddler."

a)   The term explained

The Greek term translated "troublesome meddler" (*allotrioepiskopos*) occurs only here in the New Testament. Some other verses help us to understand its meaning. In 1 Thessalonians 4:11 the apostle Paul says, "Make it your ambition to lead a quiet life and attend to your own business and work with your hands, just as we commanded you." We're to occupy ourselves with a trade and not be troublemakers who stir up society.

Paul also said, "We hear that some among you are leading an undisciplined life, doing no work at all, but acting like busybodies. Now such persons we command and exhort in the Lord Jesus Christ to work in quiet fashion and eat their own bread" (2 Thess. 3:11-12).

Those verses refer to the believer's conduct in society, not his intrusion into the personal matters of other people. "Troublesome meddler" (1 Pet. 4:15) is to be understood in the same sense. Specifically, it's a reference to political agitation—disruptive activity that interferes with the function and flow of government. That kind of conduct would compel the government to take action. It would be inaccurate for the meddler to view that response as persecution for his faith.

b) The term applied

A believer could become a troublemaker at his or her place of employment. If he or she works for a secular company and tries to force Christian standards into company policy, that might disrupt the harmony of working conditions. We need to be certain our testimony exhibits grace to the lost.

So we each need to ask ourselves, *Why am I suffering?* We are to live virtuously by telling others about Jesus Christ, being faithful at our workplace, and being good citizens in our communities. If we try to *force* our thinking on a non-Christian culture—whether it's a corporation, a workshop, or the government—we are stepping beyond biblical boundaries. Peter emphasized we're to be models of submission "to every human institution" (1 Pet. 2:13).

B. Suffering for the Right Reasons (vv. 16-18)

1. For righteous living (v. 16)

"But if anyone suffers as a Christian, let him not feel ashamed, but in that name let him glorify God."

The early Christians spoke of themselves as the brethren, the saints, and those of "the Way." But their adversaries stigmatized them with the names "Nazarenes" and "Christians." Ironically, believers began to use "Christians" as a beloved name to identify themselves.

To "glorify God" means to praise God for the privilege of suffering for righteousness. It's a privilege because we're sharing in Christ's sufferings, adding to the weight of our eternal reward, and being strengthened by the Spirit (1 Pet. 4:12-14).

2. For spiritual cleansing (vv. 17-18)

"It is time for judgment to begin with the household of God; and if it begins with us first, what will be the outcome for those who do not obey the gospel of God? And if it is with difficulty that the righteous is saved, what will become of the godless man and the sinner?"

a) What it is

The Greek term translated "time" refers to a decisive, crucial moment—in this case, the beginning of judgment. That occurred on the cross, when all our sins were judged in Christ. For Christians that judgment also includes a chastening, testing, purifying, or cleansing but not eternal condemnation.

That "household" refers to the church is evident from other scriptures. First Peter 2:5 refers to the godly "as a spiritual house." And in 1 Timothy 3:15 the church is called "the household of God."

Although judgment *begins* with His purification of the church, it *ends* with His final condemnation of the ungodly at the great white throne judgment (Rev. 20:11-15). If God has an important and serious judgment for His children now, what will be the result of judgment on the lost in the future?

b) Why it is necessary

Ezekiel 9:6 serves as an analogy to help us understand the necessity of judgment. When God looked on the sinful people of the earth to judge them, He said, "Start [the judgment] from My sanctuary," and consequently it began "with the elders who were before the temple." His judgment separated the godly from the ungodly.

Similarly, His purging is necessary to purify and separate true believers from the false and carnal. Only a pure church will make disciples of all nations effectively.

c) Why it is preferable

It is better to endure suffering with joy now than to endure the "outcome" of eternal torment with those "who do not obey the gospel of God" (1 Pet. 4:17). Verse 18 affirms the same truth. It's a quotation from Proverbs 11:31 that's better interpreted, "If the righteous receive their due on earth, how much more the wicked and the sinner?" Although believers suffer hardships now, the agony of the lost will be greater in the eternal state: they will be cast into the lake of fire (Rev. 20:15).

The apostle Paul stated the matter this way: "[Persecution] is a plain indication of God's righteous judgment so that you may be considered worthy of the kingdom of God, for which indeed you are suffering. For after all it is only just for God to repay with affliction those who afflict you, and to give relief to you who are afflicted and to us as well when the Lord Jesus shall be revealed from heaven with His mighty angels in flaming fire, dealing out retribution to those who do not know God and to those who do not obey the gospel of our Lord Jesus. And these will pay the penalty of eternal destruction" (2 Thess. 1:5-9).

IV. ENTRUST YOURSELF TO GOD (v. 19)

"Therefore, let those also who suffer according to the will of God entrust their souls to a faithful Creator in doing what is right."

A. An Explanation About Commitment

"Therefore" indicates Peter is saying something based on his previous teaching about suffering. The Greek term translated "entrust" is a banking term that speaks of a deposit for safekeeping. It's the same word Christ used on the cross in entrusting Himself to the Father (Luke 23:46). Entrusting your soul means giving your life or being. So we're to give our lives "to a faithful Creator." That phrase occurs only here in the New Testament. "Creator" remind us we're simply giving back to God what He created, which means He is most capable of caring for our lives.

"Faithful" indicates we can trust Him because He knows what's best for us. He knows our needs and will meet them according to His promise (Phil. 4:19). While we're "doing what is right" in the midst of hostility, we are to commit ourselves to God rather than defect from Him.

B. An Example of Commitment

At age thirty Geoffrey Bull was imprisoned by Chinese Communists and held for more than three years. He was subjected to solitary confinement, starvation, threats, and brainwashing. During that time he composed a poem to serve as his prayer in the midst of his suffering (cited by Paul S. Rees, *Triumphant in Trouble*

[Westwood, N.J.: Revell, 1962], pp. 119-20). He prayed that God would not let the memory of His Word grow dim or allow him to give in to doubt, loneliness, or fear. He concluded by saying that the Lord's joy was his own, and His hope his own.

Let us all seek to have that kind of commitment!

Focusing on the Facts

1. What concern did the apostle Peter express throughout his letter? Support your answer with Scripture (see pp. 70-71).
2. Like a murderer and thief, an "evildoer" is a _____ (1 Pet. 4:15; see p. 72).
3. Explain what "a troublesome meddler" is (1 Pet. 4:15). How could that apply to a believer (see pp. 72-73)?
4. What are ways for a believer to live virtuously (see p. 73)?
5. Believers are to be models of _____ "to every human institution" (1 Pet. 2:13; see p. 73).
6. Why is it a privilege to suffer for righteousness (1 Pet. 4:12-14; see p. 74)?
7. When did the beginning of judgment for believers occur (1 Pet. 4:17)? What does that judgment also include (see p. 74)?
8. How does God's judgment end (see pp. 74-75)?
9. Why is His judgment necessary (see p. 75)?
10. Spiritual cleansing is preferable to what? Support your answer with Scripture (see p. 75).
11. What does it mean to entrust your soul (see p. 76)?
12. Why is the phrase "a faithful Creator" (1 Pet. 4:19) an encouragement for believers (see p. 76)?

Pondering the Principles

1. We are to commit our lives to God in the midst of hostility (1 Pet. 4:19). Puritan Jeremiah Burroughs spoke of that truth: "A gracious heart is contented by the melting of his will and desires into God's will and desires. . . . That is the excellence of grace: grace does not only subject the will to God, but it

melts the will into God's will, so that they are now but one will. What a sweet satisfaction the soul must have in this condition, when all is made over to God" (*The Rare Jewel of Christian Contentment* [Edinburgh: The Banner of Truth Trust, 1987], pp. 53-54). Ask the Lord for His help in melting your will into His.

2. God's judgment of believers is for their spiritual purification (1 Pet. 4:17). Jerry Bridges wrote, "God uses adversity to loosen our grip on those things that are not true fruit. A severe illness or the death of someone dear to us, the loss of material substance or the tarnishing of our reputation, the turning aside of friends or the dashing of our cherished dreams on the rocks of failure, cause us to think about what is really important in life. Position or possessions or even reputation no longer seem so important. We begin to relinquish our desires and expectations—even good ones—to the sovereign will of God. We come more and more to depend on God and to desire only that which will count for eternity. God is pruning us so that we will be more fruitful" (*Trusting God* [Colorado Springs: Navpress, 1988], pp. 180-81). Be encouraged to "know that God causes all [your trials] to work together for good" (Rom. 8:28).

Scripture Index

Topical Index